#LOVEISPROJECT

presents

the greatest love story ever told

A COLLECTION OF *love stories* FROM AROUND THE WORLD

**By Chrissie Lam,
Founder of Love Is Project**

Copyright © 2019 by Chrissie Lam
The Greatest Love Story Ever Told: *A Collection of Love Stories from Around the World*
Edit by Kristina Borza and Madison Hannah
Design by Grace Leong and Callie Lindsley
Book cover design by Gretchen Legrange
Illustrations by Sujean Rim, Amber Vittoria, Vannina Olivieri
Photography by Tommaso Riva, Zissou, Georgina Goodwin, Sean Dekkers, Anna Watts,
Danielle Rubi, Martina Orska, Mark Nicdao, Jake Morales, Raskal, Wawan Muhammad, Sara
Davis, Benjamin Conley, Khasar Sandag, Peter Prato, Tania Aranjo, Nicole Gava, Chucho Potts

Love Is Project - San Francisco, California

Printed in China

1st edition, Year of Publication, 2020

ISBN 9781734129502

www.loveisproject.co

this book is dedicated to

My family and friends,
thank you for all of your
unconditional love and
support. All of our talented
collaborators around the world.
The artisans who connect
everyone through love.

CONTENTS

Photo (left) by: Sean Dekkers, Photo (previous) by: Tommaso Riva

FOREWORD

By Bandana Tewari

"Yesterday I was clever, so I wanted to change the world. Today I am wise, so I am changing myself."
- Rumi -

We live in a change-maker world led by the audacity of individual will. The compassionate rebels. The daring contrarians. The purveyors of ingenuity, inclusivity, and integrity. You find them in every part of the globe. Although we live in a not-so-brave world of dwindling democracies, the swansong of the status quo has been sung.

There is no looking back now. In these challenging times, *The Greatest Love Story Ever Told* is being told, fearlessly, by these change-makers. And each and every person in this book is one. They know that the only thing that can stand up to our present-day crisis of consciousness is LOVE. And against all odds, they will stand by it.

In Sanskrit there is one phrase that poignantly encapsulates a social philosophy, that all of humanity is made of *one* life energy: *Vasudhaiva Kutum Bakam*, or, The Whole World is One Family. It is entrenched in the ideals of compassion and inter-dependence that finds its source in the futility of isolation. It is said: "If the whole ocean is one, how then is a drop of the ocean different from the ocean? If the drop is different from the ocean, how then can it ultimately be dissolved in the ocean?" This is the philosophy of life. It is the wisdom of universal love. Just imagine the power of our interconnectedness like millions of lightning bolts that create a surge of earth consciousness. When we believe in this collective power of love, we honor the absolute sacredness of creation. All of creation.

For me personally, love is pure energy. To explain this briefly, I will dip again into the wisdom of Sanskrit, an ancient language of wise seers—secular, pragmatic and profound in equal measure.

The phrase that is used is *Aham Brahmasmi*, meaning, I Am Energy. It is the ultimate principle of non-duality. It means I am the creator *and* the creation. Consider this: Every animate and inanimate entity in this universe has the same basic chemical elements. Your iPhone, your frangipani blossom, your car, the trees in your garden, your friends who live on different continents, the distant stars and planets that roam the midnight sky, are an arrangement of the same ingredients—hydrogen, carbon, oxygen, iron, calcium, zinc, copper and so on. It is the same energy of creation or love for life, that created you and me. If we all believed in this energy, then there is no dualism; there is no *me* and the *other*. The cosmos is in me and I am the cosmos. *Aham Brahmasmi!*

What my dear friend, Chrissie Lam, founder of Love Is Project, and curator of this extraordinary book—a joyful treatise of love—knows in her heart, doesn't require my unnecessary philosophical banter. She stays true to her magic. She *lives* this energy of love effortlessly, floating from country to country, as freely as a dandelion that rides the wind, pausing occasionally to plant the seeds when a profound stillness overtakes her. She believes that love is a law unto itself. And that law is sacred. She once told me, "Love is respect for the world we inhabit *together*, not alone."

"Be universal in your Love. You will see the Universe as picture of your own Being."

Sri Chinmoy
CHITTAGONG, BANGLADESH

Bandana Tewari is a lifestyle journalist, sustainable activist, and the former editor-at-large at Vogue India. Tewari now serves as Special Advisor to Global Fashion Agenda, a jury member of H&M Foundation's Global Change Award and is a regular contributor to The Business of Fashion.

love is
the answer.

OUR LOVE STORY

"What starts out little can become big."
- Fred Rogers -

I think about this Fred Rogers quote when looking back at the past five years since starting Love Is Project. A kernel of an idea, and a modest little bracelet, have created jobs for thousands, supported communities around the world, and inspired others to spread more love. How cool and crazy is that? If you can inspire thousands, you can in turn, change the lives of millions.

A stranger once said to me, "Love is proportional to your will." The stronger your will, the bigger your love. I had just started the trip of a lifetime in St. Petersburg, Russia, when these words began to take on a life of their own.

We all agree that the world can feel wildly messy, violent, polarizing, and discouraging at times. But in every country, school, institution, community, or relationship there is one thing that always helps us to thrive: *love*. Relatable to every being in this world, LOVE is the common thread that connects us all. Love changes lives and brings people closer together. *The Greatest Love Story Ever Told* exhibits a handful of thousands of love stories collected over the past five years.

Storytelling has the power to instill empathy, shift perspectives, inspire change, and defy negativity. Every story collected is unique, personal, and yet so familiar.

Photo (left) by: Tommaso Riva

These universal stories highlight that love is family, romance, spirituality, purpose, community, acceptance, resilience and so much more—all at the same time. My hope is that these stories will inspire you to foster deeper, more meaningful connections—and to live life with an open heart.

Pictured: Enyorra, which means LOVE in Maasai

Photos by: Georgina Goodwin

Photo by: Georgina Goodwin

It all began in 2014. I was on a flight to Moscow when I struck up a conversation with two women who had just met on the plane. I asked them what love meant to them. Inspired by their openness and vulnerability, I asked to take their photo wearing a beaded bracelet designed by a woman of Kenya's Maasai tribe. This bracelet was emblazoned with the word LOVE. Fast-forward six months and 50 countries later, a collection of LOVE stories began to unfold. It was always the same question: *What does love mean to you?* After sharing stories on social media of people wearing this special bracelet, supporters around the world felt moved to get involved—and Love Is Project began to take flight.

The purpose of Love Is Project is to create jobs for artisan women in developing countries. These bracelets connect the wearer to the maker and remind us to love and be loved. Love Is Project has since grown into a global brand, providing 1,200 female artisans in 10 countries with jobs.

Seeing women around the world run their own businesses and experience financial independence is immensely rewarding, and hard to describe in words. This book encapsulates so much of what makes Love Is Project meaningful. These stories give a first-hand look at the unique cultures, talented artists, and inspiring people who teach us what it means to love.

Because you are reading this book, you are granting a new kind of freedom to artisans all over the world. You are supporting global economic empowerment, steady employment, fair wages, educational opportunities, and charitable donations. This book directly helps fund future partnerships with female artisans around the world, so we can continue to pay it forward. From the bottom of my heart— thank you.

All my love,

Chrissie

Chrissie Lam

the power of lo

e unites us all

love is
purpose.

Chrissie's Story

LOVE IS PURPOSE

"Love is possibility turned into reality"
- Dominique Soguel -

In 2012, I left behind a 12 year career in corporate fashion. After working with major fashion brands the likes of American Eagle Outfitters and Abercrombie & Fitch, this career move would be a very different one. My initial goal was to connect artisans around the world with major fashion brands—thus creating sustainable jobs in underserved communities.

However, something shifted on a trip to Ngong, Kenya. There, I connected with skilled Maasai artisans. The group works to create sustainable employment for women in Kenya who hand make jewelry and handbags. Inspired by the colors and techniques used in traditional Maasai beadwork, I designed what would later be known as the first LOVE bracelet.

I left Kenya for Russia with my LOVE bracelet in hand. On my flight, I met two women—one from Uzbekistan and one from Kyrgyzstan. Inspired by the word LOVE emblazoned on my wrist, a conversation ensued. With it, the age-old question arose: What does love mean to you? I then did something that would quickly catapult me to the center of the fashion philanthropy world—I shared the conversation on Instagram.

What started as a passion project quickly went viral. Posts about the LOVE bracelet attracted hundreds of thousands of likes on Instagram. An Indiegogo campaign designed to raise capital for the creation of a LOVE bracelet line far exceeded its original goal. Corporate partnerships with American Eagle Outfitters and Whole Foods Market led to the first large scale orders of LOVE bracelets. Within a year, a concept bracelet and a viral marketing campaign grew into Love Is Project.

Leaving a stable corporate job was initially scary, and has had its ups and downs over the years—but it has also enabled me to merge my passions for design and development together into a new category of fashion philanthropy. LOVE became my purpose.

ZULAI + SHAHLO

We all just met sitting next to each other on an Aeroflot flight to Moscow. They were the first people I shot.

> *"Love is acceptance."*
>
> Zulai
> KYRGYZSTAN (PICTURED: LEFT)

> *"Love is two people never giving up on each other."*
>
> Shahlo
> UZBEKISTAN (PICTURED: RIGHT)

Photo (clockwise from left) by: Chrissie Lam, Georgina Goodwin, Sean Dekkers, Chucho Potts, Martina Orska

EMMANUEL JAL

Emmanuel was a child soldier in Sudan. He shares his experiences with others through storytelling and performing, with the goal of creating global conscious awakening through the arts, music, writing, acting and philanthropy. His passion and purpose is to spread peace, love, justice and freedom around the world.

"Love is the art of generating positive emotions to manage your spiritual, mental and physical state. Love is complex. It can make you kill and it can make you not kill. Love can protect. It can make you jealous. It can be demanding and it can be caring. Love can be rough. Love is dangerous. Love can destroy and love can build. You gotta know what you're getting yourself involved with, because love is POWER!"

Emmanuel Jal
TONJ, SOUTH SUDAN

GILLIAN ALLAN

Gillian is a singer/musician from Glasgow, Scotland. She moved to London five years ago to pursue music.

> *"Love is music. Love is unity. It is finding something unique you share with someone—a bond. You can love in lots of different ways. Music unites people. It allows you to live in the moment, if you can capture that bond with your audience."*

Gillian Allan
GLASGOW, SCOTLAND

FREDRIK HANSEN

Fredrik, pictured with his family, is one of the founders of Roskilde, the biggest music festival in Europe.

> *"Love is sharing and caring. Love is fuel for life. Love is social responsibility Love is global caring. Love is a matter of difference."*

Fredrik Hansen
COPENHAGEN, DENMARK

Photos by: Chrissie Lam

RAABIA HAWA

Born and raised in Kenya, Raabia lost six of her friends to poachers. She founded Walk With Rangers, an organization that works on behalf of ranger welfare. In 2014, Raabia walked from Arusha, Tanzania to Nairobi, Kenya to raise awareness about these issues.

"Love is acceptance. Love is accepting every living thing and every person... regardless of species, color or tribe."

Raabia Hawa
NAIROBI, KENYA

Photos by: Georgina Goodwin

AMBER VITTORIA

Amber is an illustrator living and working in New York City; her work focuses on the accurate portrayal of women within art. She has collaborated with like-minded brands, such as Gucci, *The New York Times*, and Instagram, on pieces that further this narrative.

@ amber_vittoria

"Since I was young, creating art has been the most accurate way for me to express my thoughts, emotions, and dreams, which is why I quickly fell in love with it. Illustrating allows me to be my happiest, most honest self. I love that I can be myself within what I do and turn that into visual art. Creating art has allowed me to connect with so many individuals across the globe and make new friends."

Amber Vittoria
NEW YORK, NEW YORK, USA

#loveisproject

ALEJANDRA CARRILLO-MUÑOZ

"Love is the universal language we all understand."

Alejandra Carrillo-Muñoz
JALISCO, MEXICO

CHUCHO POTTS

Chucho is a photographer based in Mexico.

"My name is Jesus, better known as Chuchopotts. My passion for photography was born because I wanted to express what I can't through words. What is love? It is the question that perhaps has a different meaning for each person. For me, it is the best thing that can exist. Love makes you want to share with others. What I loved most about this project is that it includes people from all over the world expressing their love for what they do through bracelets full of life and color.

The artisans are the best, they make everything with LOVE! I remember the women from Tilcajete, always smiling, carving and painting bracelets with their hands. They were shy, but proud that their handicrafts would travel the world and be a part of a gift of love to the world."

Chucho Potts

OAXACA, MEXICO

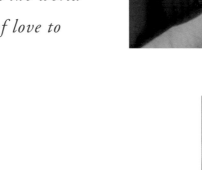

SAMARA

"Love is when someone's happiness instantly puts the most genuine smile on your face, no matter what."

Samara

OAXACA, MEXICO

Photo (previous) by: Anna Watts,
Photos (current/next page):
Chucho Potts

ROJ SANGKASABA

"Love is a feeling and energy… what you project toward others. Love is passion."

Roj Sangkasaba
BANGKOK, THAILAND

JENN HADI

Jenn is a PADI Scuba Instructor based in Indonesia.

"Love always protects. As divers, we are the ambassador of the ocean. This time we had the opportunity to witness hundreds of hammerheads, the elusive sharks of Banda Sea. We're hoping more people will take the opportunity to experience this magical encounter in order to spread awareness and help protect their habitat. You can't love and protect what you don't know."

Jenn Hadi
BANDA SEA, INDONESIA

Photo (left) by: Nicole Gava

SARA DAVIS

Meet Sara. She is one of the talented photographers who captures magical moments for Love Is Project.

Photos by: Sara Davis

> *"I can't wait to see where my creativity and passion for light and images takes me. I am so excited to be photographing 'authentic love relationships' for Love Is Project. I hope that my images help to promote the women this project serves. To me, love is seeing the beauty that exists in everyone and fostering that beauty to shine."*

Sara Davis

SAN FRANCISCO, CALIFORNIA, USA

PAM + JEREMY BEETON

After seven months of pregnancy, Pam's water broke early. This photo was taken while she was on bed rest before baby Willoughby came into the world on June 21, 2017.

> *"Love is the most powerful force on the planet. Love can heal. Love can inspire and motivate. It is a force to be reckoned with. Love is purpose. We can't wait to share this kind of love with our little girl."*

The Beetons

SAN FRANCISCO, CALIFORNIA, USA

MARTINA ORSKA

Martina is a photographer based in Quito, Ecuador.

"I believe that developing ideas through the language of creativity is one of the most wonderful things an artist can experience. The transformation of a concept into an image is the way in which my essence is portrayed. Andean surrealism, mysticism and an indigenous worldview are constant factors that have marked my documentary photography. Ideas for personal projects are born directly from my dreams and guts. These are stories produced by an internal monologue, where silence, effectively, is the loudest sound.

It was wonderful to be a small part of Love is Project. I loved being able to take photographs of the women who are behind the LOVE bracelets. It was a unique experience where I got to see a tiny bit of a day in their lives—how they laugh, how they make jokes, how they support each other, how they work, and especially how they welcomed us into their lives. I went back to Quito with a huge smile on my face!"

Martina Orska

QUITO, ECUADOR

Photos by: Martina Orska

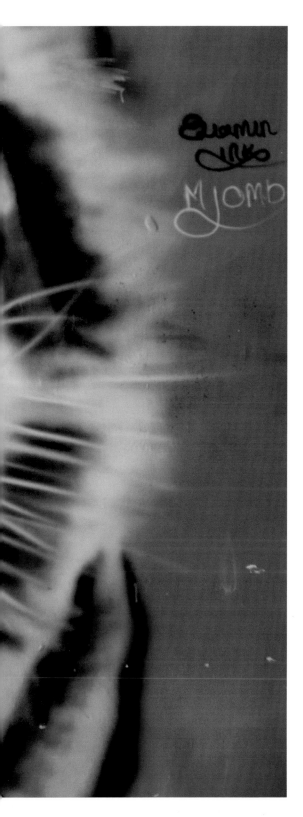

ELIAMIN

We had the pleasure of visiting Nairobi-based artist, Eliamin, at his speakeasy tattoo parlor and Matatu bus graffiti garage. He rose from humble beginnings to create a life filled with purpose and love. He is passionate about connecting with and helping others. He's now collaborating with his childhood friend, G. He has always admired G's artistic skills at school, and was thrilled to reconnect with him years later.

> *"Love is a great interest and pleasure in something. Love connects people, builds trust, and unites. I love what I do because it gives me the happiness and freedom to create with different people every day."*

Eliamin
NAIROBI, KENYA

love is
global

LOVE IS GLOBAL

"The planet does not need more successful people. The planet desperately needs more peacemakers, healers, restorers, storytellers, and lovers of all kinds."
- Dalai Lama -

There isn't anything more universal than love. Showing the power of love across different cultures has been the foundation of Love Is Project. What follows is a taste of my travel highlights and collaborations with photographers around the world in a quest to understand the meaning of love, in all its diverse forms.

ORIGINAL TRAVELS

Russia, Mongolia, Latvia,
Lithuania, Poland, Hungary,
Croatia, Serbia, Bulgaria, Turkey,
Georgia, Armenia, Jordan, Cyprus,
Israel, Palestine, Lebanon, UAE,
South Korea, Indonesia, Borneo,
Brunei, Singapore, Sri Lanka,
Nepal, Bangladesh, Thailand,
Myanmar, China, Japan, UK,
France, Kenya, USA

ADDITIONAL COUNTRIES
REPRESENTED

Belarus, Netherlands, Costa Rica,
Germany, Italy, Australia, Canada,
Syria, Chile, Sudan, Uzbekistan,
New Zealand, Spain, Krygystan,
Belarus, Nigeria, Denmark,
South Africa

WHERE OUR ARTISANS LIVE

India, Bhutan, Ecuador, Mexico,
Guatemala, Colombia, Philippines
Vietnam, Indonesia, Kenya

Photographer Spotlight

KHASAR SANDAG

I wanted to be a documentary filmmaker growing up because documentaries reveal life on Earth. They have no script and are genuine. However, when I went to university in 1996, I bailed on my childhood dream because I didn't think I could live off movie-making in Mongolia at the time. Instead, I chose the most logical career path at that moment. Mongolia was a new democracy and had opened its doors to business and capital. So, I chose to study international business.

After working government agencies, private businesses, international financial institutions and a multinational company, I came to the conclusion that the only thing I didn't do is work for myself and love my work. At 34, I quit my day job and became a documentary photographer. This is the closest I could come to my dream job of documentary filmmaking.

Photos by: Khasar Sandag

BATMUNKH

Batmunkh is a 19-year-old camel herder from Central Mongolia.

"Love is trust and respect."

Batmunkh
TUV PROVINCE,
MONGOLIA

I met Chrissie a few years back in Mongolia while she was on her journey through various countries. She had a dream of making meaningful, inclusive products and wanted to create change in the supply chains of distant and exotic lands.

This struck a note with me, because love is such a wonderful thing to give, share, and experience. It is very intimate, yet people were happy to share their thoughts on it. Being able to share what love is for Mongolians is a privilege for me, because I get to showcase my people, my country and their love through my photos. Come visit Mongolia—a land of wonderful people, magical landscapes, and a place where you truly feel freedom.

Khasar specializes in environmental portraits and social documentaries. His work has been featured in Time magazine and on Apple billboards. While not on assignment, he runs the only local film production service in Mongolia, Steppe Fixers Mongolia.

AIMULDER

Aimulder lives in Bayan-Ulgii Province, where the Kazakh Eagle Hunters originate. She is keeping the 4,000 year old tradition alive as an eagle huntress in-training.

*"Love is
eagle hunting."*

Aimulder
BAYAN-ULGII PROVINCE,
SAGSAI TOWN, MONGOLIA

Photo by: Khasar Sandag

Photo by: Khasar Sandag

GANTUMUR

Winters are long, hard, and cold on the Mongolian steppe. Families are nomadic herders and live in yurts.

"Love is spring because it's the time I get to play with baby lambs and goats."

Gantumur
MONGOLIAN STEPPE,
MONGOLIA

MY PHUN

My Phun is from the Padaung tribe. They wear metal neck coils starting at the age of eight, increasing the number as they age. She has 25 coils, the maximum number. Legend has it that the coils serve as protection from tigers.

"Love is many things. I love having people come from around the world to visit me at Inie Lake."

My Phun
INIE LAKE, MYANMAR

Photo (left) by: Anna Watts, Photo (top): Ryan Lawton

CATALINA GOMEZ

"Love is your soul's recognition in another."

Catalina Gomez
LAKE ATITLAN, GUATEMALA

Photo by: Chrissie Lam

JOAN

Joan is a vintage fashion dealer in Brick Lane, Shoreditch. Her family is from Nigeria. She loves London for its culture and the arts.

> *"Love is humanity... people showing love for each other."*
>
> Joan
> LONDON, ENGLAND

GRETA EAGAN

Greta is founder and CEO of Beauty Scripts.

> *"Love is the unseen energy that connects us all and is best felt when we take care of others as we would ourselves."*
>
> Greta Eagan
>
> JACKSON HOLE, WYOMING, USA

Photos by: Chrissie Lam

RAKAN

Rakan is a member of the Bedouin police force.

> *"Love is something you want, but is sometimes difficult to get."*
>
> Rakan
>
> JAFAR, JORDAN

Photo by: Tommaso Riva

"No one is born hating another person because of the colour of his skin, or his background, or his religion. People must learn to hate, and if they can learn to hate, they can be taught to love, for love comes more naturally to the human heart than its opposite."

Nelson Mandela
MVEZO, SOUTH AFRICA

love is romance.

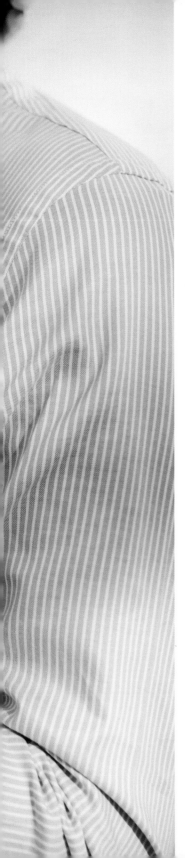

Photo by: Martina Orska

LOVE IS ROMANCE

"Love is growing together as individuals."

- Amy Lippincott -

When people told me their stories of romantic love, I didn't hear about the fairy tale version of love—the "butterflies-in-my-stomach" narrative we're accustomed to hearing. What sparked the romances ranged wildly—from a childhood friendship to a Facebook message. But what resulted was a story about being changed and inspired— by a first love or a love story spanning an entire lifetime. These are stories about the life changing power of finding *your person.*

Photos by: Anna Watts

JEROEN JACOBS
+ LAUREN HEFFRON

Lauren and I met each other nine years ago when I was studying abroad at the University of Wisconsin - Madison. I was with friends at a popular college bar when I noticed a beautiful girl across the room. I leaned over to my friend to point her out and it turned out that he knew her. He got to his feet, walked over to her, and introduced me to Lauren.

When I left the US to return home (I am from the Netherlands), the two of us stayed very close. We tried to remain friends even though it became clear to each of us that we would not be able to get over one another. Lauren flew to Amsterdam a few years later on Christmas and from that point forward, we knew it would be forever.

"... and from that point forward, we knew it would be forever."
Jeroen Jacobs
NEW YORK, NEW YORK, USA

After a long-distance relationship we ended up in New York City, where we currently live together. About one and a half years ago, we were traveling through Guatemala when we met Chrissie and Anna, who were shooting photos for Love is Project. Chrissie asked if we wanted to be hand models and we were happy to help. It resulted in a very fun morning with great photos!

When I was planning to propose to Lauren over the summer, I reached out to Chrissie and Anna because I knew Anna lived in New York City and I hoped that she could take pictures on the day of our engagement! Anna was so kind for wanting to help. One and a half years after meeting each other in a remote part of Guatemala, we met again in Manhattan just after I proposed to Lauren.

We spent about two hours on our rooftop and in the city taking pictures. It was a wonderful afternoon and a great way to memorialize that special day.

EMILIEN PONS + JENN BERETTA

Emilien and Jenn have known each other since they were five years old. Jenn moved away at the age of seven and they randomly reconnected again at age twenty. They now have a son together named Leo.

"Love is about being in the right place at the right time."

Emilien Pons
ANNECY, FRANCE

"Love is a thread of trust, respect understanding, and magic!"

Jenn Beretta
ANNECY, FRANCE

ASHLIE ARTHUR + NOEL RIVARD

"Love is a oneness between people; to care for another in a way that is comparable to caring for yourself. You can't have a strong attachment without sharing yourself and the other person sharing themselves."

Ashlie Arthur
WYOMING, USA

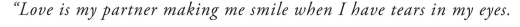

Photo (clockwise from top-left)
by: Chrissie Lam, Raskal,
Sara Davis

STÉPHANIE CHEVIER + DEVON ASH

"Love is my partner making me smile when I have tears in my eyes.
Love is being surrounded by community, heart wide open, listening
as they share all the ways I matter to them.
Love is walking through my neighbourhood and stopping to watch
the bees with the flowers.
Love is laughing with my sister.
Love is a morning coffee made while I sleep.
Love is choosing every moment to live this life as an artist.
Love is keeping my body hydrated and nourished.
Love is coming home to a hot bath with the man I adore.
Love is laughing my way through this beautiful life.

Stéphanie Chevier
VANCOUVER, CANADA

ELVIS + JILLIAN

Jillian and Elvis met when Jillian posted a Craigslist ad looking for a tour guide around Chicago. Even though her request was platonic, she had several stipulations around gender, height and age, even asking for a photo to be included in the application. Elvis found her request hilarious and intriguing, so he wrote her stating that he did not meet the criteria and would not be sending a photo. Instead, he described himself as having a peg-leg and an eyepatch. They chatted online for three to four hours every day before they finally started speaking on the phone. It was another five months before they would meet. Elvis describes their first meeting as "supernatural" and knew that she was the one for him.

Photo by: Sara Davis

"Love is not about you, it's about us."

Elvis
CHICAGO, ILLINOIS, USA

"Love is...
Unconditional.
Understanding.
Uninhibited.
Unexplainable."

Jillian
CHICAGO, ILLINOIS, USA

AIDA AQUINO BOYO + CRISTINO LAVARIEGA

Aida and Cristino are Mexican artisans. They create Love Is Project Corazon bracelets. Aida is a painter and Cristino is a craftsman. Aida and her husband met when she was working as a housekeeper in a house he was renting.

"Amor es todo."

["Love is everything."]

Aida Aquino Boyo

OAXACA, MEXICO

Photos by: Chucho Potts

"Si tu das amor, amor recibes."

["If you give love,

you receive love."]

Cristino Lavariega

OAXACA, MEXICO

JURE KNEZEVIC + TIFFANY BLUM

Newlyweds, Jure, from Croatia, and Tiffany from the United States.

"Essentially, there are only two emotions; love, and fear. Everything else is a derivative. And you can always choose, so choose love."

Jure Knezevic
DUBUQUE, IOWA, USA

"Love is believing in and seeing the good in people and forgiving their flaws and mistakes. Love is realizing that we are all connected and here together and that we are meant to live and work as one! Love is love."

Tiffany Blum
DUBUQUE, IOWA, USA

Photos by: Sara Davis

Photo by: Zissou

ONSI AND GLADYS LAM

My parents, Onsi and Gladys, celebrating 45 years of marriage. They met in San Francisco after my mom got dressed in the dark and raced to the bus stop. There, my dad pointed out she was wearing two different colored shoes. They have been together ever since.

I appreciate all their help and support of me—especially during the startup phase of Love Is Project. It truly has been a labor of love.

"Love is an emotion…
it can be fleeting
or lasting."

Gladys Lam
SAN FRANCISCO, CALIFORNIA, USA

JAMES BEVERIDGE + JUDITH LESSER

"Love is bringing the best out of each other and seeing the good things in the other that they don't always see in themselves. Love is encouraging growth. Love is a journey."

Judith Lesser

BROOKLYN, NEW YORK, USA

SAM ROGERS + JAIME DARROW

"Love is a ray of sunshine amid the darkest of storms."

Sam Rogers

BROOKLYN, NEW YORK, USA

Photo (left) by: Jean Laurent Gaudy, Photo (top) by: Nicole Welch

I do weddings too!

CHRISSIE LAM

You already know I love love. But here's one thing you might not know about me: I've been honored to officiate three weddings for dear friends. There's a certain magic to being a guest and witness to the love between two people—but being the one to actually tell their love story in front of family and friends, and preside over their legal commitment to one another? That's transcendent.

The first wedding I officiated was for my childhood friend James and his wife Judith, which took place in the vaulted room of a quirky St. Louis museum. It was the perfect setting for sharing the funny story of how I met the soon-to-be bride and groom, which involved finding the two of them on the roof of my New York City apartment.

Since that meeting, I was hooked on their love for each other and their love of travel—stories we shared with all of their guests during the ceremony. Judith and James couldn't get enough of me and even spent part of their honeymoon with me in Bali!

Personal anecdotes and common interests as allegories for married life found their way into the second wedding I officiated for my food-loving cousin, Leslie, and her food-fanatic husband, Dan. The setting? A beautiful Japanese tea garden. And the most recent wedding I officiated was on a rooftop in Williamsburg with my friend Jaime and her husband Sam, who have an undying love for Bruce Springsteen. It goes without saying that wedding number three had its fair share of Boss quotes.

love is
family.

LOVE IS FAMILY

"Like the seaweed that clings to each other after each passing boat separates them, so too a family will come together with the passing of each crisis."

- Indonesian Proverb -

For many around the world, family is the nucleus of life—the sun around which all other forms of love orbit. Mothers have told me how family gives them a true sense of purpose. Children described even the smallest acts of familial love with a sense of wonder.

In war-torn lands, family was described to me as the only constant. After hearing hundreds of definitions of love, one response has always stood out as the most popular of all: love is family.

CHRIS THOMPSON

Chris with his wife Joanne, and children, Chayton and Chanoa.

> *"Love is simply being kind: Kindness to ourselves in how we nurture our physical and spiritual bodies; to those around us as we show patience and unconditional understanding; to our community and how we offer a helping hand; to our environment in how we respect nature and all living beings; to the world in understanding that we are all perfectly imperfect. Be kind. That is love."*

Chris Thompson

BALI, INDONESIA

LIBERATO + AMPARO

Liberato and Amparo have been together for 38 years. They met making sombreros in Tuchin. She wove the straps and he bought them from her. For them, love is family. They have worked hard to educate their three sons and three daughters. They are blessed with 12 grandchildren.

"El amor es la familia."
["Love is family."]

Liberato + Amparo
TUCHIN, COLOMBIA

Photos by: Anna Watts

HEIDI BLAIR

"Being a mom is my higher purpose. It is the definition of unconditional love and the compass from which I navigate. I consider it the highest privilege and life's most precious gift."

Heidi Blair
BALI, INDONESIA

TIM FIJAL

Tim with his son and daughter. They are the founders of TRI Upcycle.

> *"The best thing about being a dad is that daily call you get to love selflessly— to give without taking. It's not always easy, but it nurtures a humble heart and ultimately brings shine to one's soul."*

Tim Fijal

BALI, INDONESIA

ISABELLA BRANSON

"Love is family."

Isabella Branson
WINCHESTER, UNITED KINGDOM

HEA WON HARRIS + HARPER HARRIS

"In many ways she is my soul mate and teacher. She reminds me to not rush and to be in the moment. She is pure love and compassion. Her kindness and love is not judgemental. She is what it means to be human!"

Hea Won Harris
ATLANTA, GEORGIA, USA

GRACE CHANG + ODIN SUN

"I love my mom because she plays basketball with me. She is always the only mom on the court. She does everything with me! We are buds. We love each other."

Odin Sun
NEW YORK, NEW YORK, USA

STEFANIE, MAX + DJANGO JENCQUEL

Stefanie and Max expecting the arrival of Django in December 2014 (pictured left).

"Love is all we need to be happy."

Stefanie

BALI, INDONESIA

"Love means sharing and caring."

Django

BALI, INDONESIA

Photos by: Tommaso Riva

MADE + ITA

Made and Ita are a Love Is Project mother-daughter team in Bali and Java, Indonesia. They have been able to expand the size of their physical workshop with our orders since we started working with them in 2017. They have had this business for 20 years and learned how to bead from books.

> *"Love is the meaning of everything...Love is what it means to be human."*
>
> Ita
>
> BALI, INDONESIA

DENDI SHERPA

Dendi Sherpa met his wife, Mingma Chamiji Sherpa, on Facebook. After a month of dating, they got married. After nine years of marriage, they now have two kids. I was invited to their home for a very Buddhist Christmas and shared a delicious home cooked meal with his family. His son, Pasang Tenji Sherpa, is quite the soccer player and now an avid Angry Birds fan thanks to my friend, Sandra. "Pasang" means Friday. Sherpas are named after the day of the week they are born. To Dendi, love is his family and happiness.

"Ma tapai lai maya gar chu."
["I love you"]
Dendi Sherpa
KATHMANDU, NEPAL

Photo (top) by: Chrissie Lam
Photo (right) by: Sandra Keller

ODESSA

> *"Love is holding all of me."*
>
> Odessa
> AUSTIN, TEXAS, USA

Photo (left) by: Tomasso Riva, Photo (below) by: Zissou

BADGER BARING

Badger left his finance job in England to pursue a career in furniture design.

> *"Love is my daughter, Nilaya."*
>
> Badger Baring
> BALI, INDONESIA

BUD HART

Love is home for Bud—which is how Bali made him feel during his first visit in 1998. Yearly visits were not enough, so he left his New York City psychotherapy practice in 2005 to move here.

Love Is Project was launched from Hartland Villa. Bud Hart and his staff are like family and their villa has served as a beautiful backdrop for numerous photo shoots.

Photos by: Tommaso Riva

"Expansion is the essence of objectless desire. Desire seeks to create. Creativity seeks to expand and grow for its own sake."

Bud Hart

BALI, INDONESIA

NYOMAN

Nyoman puts love into every meal she makes, so that others can receive her love. After tasting a delicious meal years ago, she taught herself how to cook. She has worked as a private chef for over 20 years and is known for her famous homemade mango pie.

"Love is cooking."

Nyoman

BALI, INDONESIA

PABLO

> *"Papa et fils ont le même collier/bracelet !*
> *Vous aimez?"*
> *["Dad and son have the same collar/bracelet!*
> *You like?"]*
>
> Pablo
> PARIS, FRANCE

Photos (clockwise from above) by: Ivan Kricak, Sandra Keller, Sabine Spruyt Godon

MILES DAVIS

"My name is Miles Davis. I am six years old and live in Washington, DC. I'm a Welsh Terrier, so technically I'm from Wales, U.K. I am innately curious and constantly learning new things, but one thing I know for sure is that I love my pack. I also love a good meatball, my beat up red tennis ball, giving hugs and singing (believe it or not, I know how to sing). My aunt, Sandra, told me about Love is Project and it didn't take much convincing to get me in their new collar. Not only is it sharp (and I think I look pretty darn good in it), but I'm able to share an important reminder every time I wear it—that love is limitless, non-discriminatory, and universal. Love is a powerful force that can be communicated by feeling. I am grateful to feel and give love every single day."

Miles Davis
WASHINGTON DC, USA

FELICE

"Love is life. Life is sharing and spreading positive vibes, forgiving and trusting, helping with out judging, and spending precious moments together."

Felice
PARIS, FRANCE

CAMILLE JUCO + CÚ

"Love is 'Better Together'
playing on the car stereo as
you drive down the coast."
Camille Juco
MANILA, PHILIPPINES

"Love is jumping into the
pool with my hoomans on a
hot summer day."
Cú (Golden Retriever)
MANILA, PHILIPPINES

MARTY

"I ♥ LOVE! To me, love means
everlasting, unlimited, unconditional
affection, licks and loyalty. And lamb!"
Marty
SAN FRANCISCO, CALIFORNIA, USA

Photo (left) by: Ryan Lawton, Photo (below) provided by: Natalia Ditto

VALENTINO

Shelter dog, Valentino, was rescued by Ryan Lawton.

"Love is a forever home."
Valentino
PALM SPRINGS, CALIFORNIA, USA

NATALIA DITTO + LOKI

"We love Loki because he's family. Love to him means protecting his family, always being close and showering us all with licks. The excitement he wakes up with each morning is contagious."
Natalia Ditto
BROOKLYN, NEW YORK, USA

love is in the everyday.

Photo by: Georgina Goodwin

LOVE IS IN THE EVERYDAY

"If you look for it, I've got a sneaky feeling you'll find that love actually is all around."

- Love Actually -

Each morning, we wake up prepared to take on a new day. We anticipate routine and mundane-filled moments, but then sometimes we are overwhelmed by unexpected bursts of everyday wonder.

Maybe it's a sudden awareness of blooming flowers or just appreciating that first sip of morning coffee—one thing is certain, love can be found anywhere and everywhere.

Photos by: Georgina Goodwin

SHEILA NDINDI

"Love is caring and forgiving. Love makes the world a better place."

Sheila Ndindi

NAIROBI, KENYA

JAN BUCO

"Love is giving away the last slice of food when you're really hungry."

Jan Buco

MANILA, PHILIPPINES

Photo by: Mark Nicdao

PRADEEP WIJEKOON

Pradeep is a Tuk Tuk taxi driver.

> *"Love is like a Tuk Tuk, it can take you everywhere and it is very strong."*
>
> Pradeep Wijekoon
> KANDY, SRI LANKA

DANIELA TRUJILLO

> *"Love is movement. It's what moves you and inspires you to do things—to keep going. It's not only to love one person, but to love to be alive and love yourself. It's waking up every day and wanting to do whatever makes you happy. Love is what moves us."*
>
> Daniela Trujillo
> LAKE ATITLAN, GUATEMALA

TATJANA LIEPELT

"There are many reasons to love, it doesn't have to be a person, it can be a moment, it can be dancing to vinyl after the worst day, it can be getting on your board and letting the ocean take you away from whatever is going on ... it's finding a moment."

Tatjana Liepelt

SANTA MONICA, CALIFORNIA, USA

MARCO + SIMONETTA LASTRUCCI

Italians, Marco and Simonetta, have lived in Bali for 17 years. They are the founders of Quarzia textiles and fashion, which designs unique batiks.

"Love is the most important feeling you can have as a human being."

Marco Lastrucci

BALI, INDONESIA

"Love is the simple things. It is the joy of being where I am and who I am—centered and grounded and happy to do my work."

Simonetta Lastrucci

BALI, INDONESIA

Photos (clockwise from top) by: Benjamin Conley, Zissou, Anna Watts, Chrissie Lam

AMISHA PATEL

*"Love is seeing
and being seen."*

Amisha Patel
NEW YORK,
NEW YORK, USA

Photos by: Tommaso Riva

LUCIA GUTIERREZ

"Love is a connection, the force that keeps us all going—getting up every morning, putting one foot in front of the other, doing our best. I feel it more when I'm in nature, or when a stranger smiles at me."

Lucia Gutierrez

SAN JOSE, COSTA RICA

SAN TONG

"Love is everything. It's the air we breathe and hugs that engulf us. It's desire, yearning, patience, sleepless nights, physical sacrifice, smiles, joy, and sometimes heartache and loss. It's a feeling of being at home and bathing in warmth and welcome arms. It's unconditional and should be the fabric of every being."

San Tong

VENICE BEACH, CALIFORNIA, USA

Photo by: Chrissie Lam

STIRLING ACAPELLA VOCAL GROUP

I met the Stirling Acapella Vocal Group from East London, South Africa on a bus ride to Lithuania. They were competing at the World Choir Games. I was even treated to a private concert on the bus!

> *"Love is music. When different cultures and nations can come together and be united as one through music, love among each other crosses boundaries. No longer do we see each other as different, but all are the same with a common cause."*
> Stirling Acapella Vocal Group
> EAST LONDON, SOUTH AFRICA

WILLY CHAVARRIA

Long-time friend, Willy, is an endless source of inspiration and laughs to me. He started a menswear fashion brand which mixes his cholo roots with traditional American workwear.

"Love is giving. Love is inspiring others to love. Love is the answer to every question. Love is knowing that there is purpose...and that purpose is simply to give love. Love is what we are when everything else disappears. Love is what keeps the blood in our veins warm. Love is free of words and fashion and even emotion. Love is all of us together at once inside a sparkling, radiating star with our eyes closed, smiling and holding each other."

Willy Chavarria

NEW YORK, NEW YORK, USA

Photos by: Chrissie Lam

SUJEAN RIM

Sujean is a freelance illustrator, designer and consultant with a focus in fashion, accessories, lifestyle and children's industries. She is also an author and illustrator of several published Children's Books. She lives in New York with her husband and their son, and is a big believer in LOVE.

> *"Love is the precious life force of everything. It's what connects us to the universe and to each other."*
> Sujean Rim
> NEW YORK, NEW YORK, USA

PALOMA AZPURUA

"Love is infinite.
Love is here and now."

Paloma Azpurua
CARACAS, VENEZUELA

Photo (left) by: Pablo Naranjo, Photo (right) by Wawan Muhammad

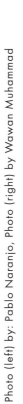

SOL ZURITA

"Love is everything! I think it is
the only thing that really matters."

Sol Zurita
QUITO, ECUADOR

KETUT

Ketut is a surf photographer based in Bali.

> *"Love is Bali."*
> Ketut
> BALI, INDONESIA

XENIA KELSCH

Xenia of Germany lives in Bali and has her own swimwear line called Makara.

> *"Love is passion in everything you do. Love is everywhere."*
> Xenia Kelsch
> BALI, INDONESIA

SIMON PALMER

Simon and his wife started One Love in Bali.

"Love is beyond words."

Simon Palmer
BALI, INDONESIA

Photographer Spotlight

ZISSOU

Without love, we are without hope, security, and purpose. Every day that we allow love to drive our decision making is a better day.

A serendipitous meeting with Chrissie a few years back offered me the opportunity to take some photographs of my friends wearing the original LOVE bracelet. As Chrissie interviewed them, I listened to their stories of love and realized this project was about so much more than a bracelet. It is about reminding each and every one of us just how important love should be in guiding our thoughts.

Zissou is a creative polymath based in Bali. Having worked across the breadth of creative industries over the years, it was not until his arrival in Indonesia that he found his calling.

love is community.

LOVE IS COMMUNITY

"If you want to go quickly, go alone.
If you want to go far, go together."
- African proverb -

They say it takes a village to raise a child. I think no matter our age, we are all still children raised by our communities. Who we are at home, work, and in our relationships is a result of the community we surround ourselves with.

After engaging with communities all over the world, I've learned that there is no limit to how much a community can feed the heart and soul.

SAMMY SEMAT

Sammy is a Maasai community leader. He is pictured above with his wife, Martha, son, Dylan Lemayian, and daughter, Ben Sabdhio.

> *"Love Is Project creates employment opportunities that uplift my community in Ngong Hills, Kenya, empowering women and their families. These earnings have funded 60 students' secondary school attendance over the past three years and allowed 150 women to invest in each other through other income-generating projects."*
>
> Sammy Semat
>
> NGONG HILLS, KENYA

EMMA + BEVERLEY

Emma and Beverley are friends in California.

> *"True friends don't grow apart even though we don't talk every day!"*
> Emma + Beverley
> SANTA MONICA, CALIFORNIA, USA

Photos by: Benjamin Conley

Photo by: Anna Watts

KEYLOR SUAZO

"Love is when you give everything with all your heart without expecting anything."

Keylor Suazo
ANTIGUA, GUATEMALA

Photo by: Anna Watts

ANNA ASPENSON

Anna will go great lengths to show her love.

"I'd jump into a pit of polar bears for you. Love is sharing a unique language. It's holding someone's heart and promising to care for it"
Anna Aspenson
LAKE ATITLAN, GUATEMALA

CARESS BANSON

Feeding Metro Manila is a hunger relief charity that aims to alleviate hunger among the urban poor and at the same time address food wastage in the metropolis. Unsold food is collected daily from hotels, bakeries, markets, groceries and other establishments. It is then distributed to different marginalized communities in Metro Manila.

> *"I love feeding the hungry because it has become a constant nourishment of my spirit. A warm embrace from the poor is an assurance that love abounds. Love is collecting day-old donuts and cinnamon rolls. Love is Feeding Metro Manila."*
>
> Caress Banson
> MANILA, PHILIPPINES

Photo by: Jake Morales

A note from Chrissie

Caress and her family and friends warmly welcomed me to Manila. I saw all the incredible work they are doing with the disadvantaged youth in the slums—feeding 600 children every day. We visited one area and gave the kids LOVE bracelets. They thoughtfully gave us handwritten thank you cards in return.

ELISA HOLISA HANDAYANI

Elisa Holisa is a self-taught artisan. She employs 300 women in five villages who make Love Is Project's Unity and Friendship bracelets. Together, they produce 200 bracelets each day. The women work from home—allowing them flexibility to care for children and to attend to household chores. Their wages support over 600 children, paying for food, school fees, home upgrades, and transportation. Elisa is grateful to be able to help her community.

> *"Love is when I can make other people happy."*
> Elisa Holisa Handayani
> JAVA, INDONESIA

Photographer Spotlight

MARK NICDAO

Love is defined to me as this quote from Lao Tzu: "Kindness in words creates confidence. Kindness in thinking creates profoundness. Kindness in giving creates love." When you find your own meaning of love, without a doubt you can give love and lose love without anything in return.

Mark Nicdao is a celebrated fashion and entertainment photographer from Mamila, Philippines.

> *"Kindness in words creates confidence. Kindness in thinking creates profoundness. Kindness in giving creates love."*
>
> Lao Tzu
> CHINA

SAM SADHWANI

> *"Love for me is a lot of things and comes in many many forms. But I think above all, it's being selfless. It's putting someone or something above yourself."*
>
> Sam Sadhwani
> MANILA, PHILIPPINES

BIANCA, MARIKA + CARINA

Bianca, Marika and Carina are the founders of Grounded Philippines, an art and lifestyle brand that encourages people to live their most authentic lives. They helped organize my trip, including a photo shoot and introductions to local artisans. I don't know what I would have done without their help! They made me feel so welcomed in Manila.

"Love is eternal, it transcends time and space. Love is an absolute truth and it is the root of all that is good in the universe."

Marika Manglapus Ledesma
MANILA, PHILIPPINES

SORBELATO

Photos (previous/current page) by: Mark Nicdao

MALALA YOUSAFZAI

"I raise up my voice—not so I can shout, but so those without a voice can be heard...we cannot succeed when half of us are held back."
Malala Yousafzai
MINGORA, PAKISTAN

LUCIA GRANADOS HALLER

> *"Love is giving selflessly, love is being a team, love is having compassion, love is laughing and being silly together, love is seeing the good in everyone and everything."*
>
> Lucia Granados Haller
> MUNICH, GERMANY

Photo (clockwise from top)
by: Anna Watts, Chrissie Lam,
Martina Orska

Photographer Spotlight

GEORGINA GOODWIN

What does love mean to me? Such a huge and wonderful question! It means connection, comfort and safety, a place of belonging—home. Knowing there is something out there—LOVE—that is so perfect and also so imperfect at the same time, challenges me to be the best person I can be.

I love my work—my photographs—as it's a way to connect with people, to travel the world with the purpose of experiencing, hearing, and sharing stories of people and the environment. I love vibrant color, so my photographs are always full of color! One of my favorite memories of working with Love Is Project is when Chrissie had this incredible idea to have Maasai and Samburu jumping on a trampoline wearing LOVE bracelets. She actually found a huge trampoline and lugged it to the Ngong Hills just outside Nairobi where we did the most fun photoshoot capturing beautiful Samburu men dressed in their traditional *shuka* (blanket) and *mchanga* (beads) jumping on a trampoline for the very first time in their lives! Their faces were priceless!

> *"... [Love] means connection, comfort and safety, a place of belonging—home."*
> Georgina Goodwin
> NAIROBI, KENYA

The Samburu (and Maasai) are known for their jumping skills. When these very happy men came back down to the ground and tried to jump off the earth again, they were dismayed at how hard they found it to get any lift after experiencing what was possible on the trampoline. What a day!

I'm a passionate Aries born in Nairobi, Kenya – it's my country, my home and my huge LOVE.

In my mid-20s, I bought my first decent camera and started feeling the need to create. That need has developed into a successful and wonderful career over the last 12 years. It was while on a job, in the deepest Tanzanian bush, that I met my husband. My work took me to a place where I found the person I had been waiting for my whole life. I LOVE color, I LOVE new experiences, I LOVE the access photography allows me to our world—to travel, to hear and to share the stories of the people I meet and the places I see. It's a privilege to have the life I lead.

In 2017, I was lucky enough to visit Love Is Project artisan, Ann, and her community of Maasai women in a remote village outside of Olepolos, located over the Ngong Hills in Kenya.

We toured her new house in her *manyatta*, which is literally a home that LOVE built for her and her family. I heard firsthand how we've changed thousands of lives by providing stable jobs during drought years, allowing families to pay school fees for children and invest in other income-generating projects.

For Ann, love is being together and sharing everything. I left them with photos and touching stories from customers all over the world who wear their LOVE bracelets with pride. These moments remind me that we're creating much more than just a bracelet. Love is community.

Georgina is a contributor to Getty Images and her work has been published in the New York Times, Vogue, Elle and AFP. As an East African photojournalist, Georgina normally covers heavy topics, such as FGM, fistula, and humanitarian crises.

Photos by: Georgina Goodwin

JEREMIAH KIPAINOI

"Love is when people come together selflessly to contribute to the betterment of their communities."

Jeremiah Kipainoi
KAJIADO, KENYA

love is spirituality.

LOVE IS SPIRITUALITY

"Love is the every only god."

- E.E. Cummings -

In holy festivals, in temples, and in churches around the world, I've seen a oneness of all faiths. Even outside of traditional religious structures, many feel inspired by an energy, a force— something larger than themselves.

Whether it's attributed to a god, spirits, the Universe, or something different, all these paths of thought attempt to lead us to the same destination: love.

Photo by: Chrissie Lam

CHAITANYASHREE

Chaitanyashree is a sound healer from Nepal.

"Love is a blessing flowing from the divine to light the soul. Love is a sound, a vibration, a frequency, and energy. Love is the fragrance of the heart."

Chaitanyashree

KATHMANDU, NEPAL

LOIS DAVIS

"Love is asking the Lord to be with us through this day and help us to see the good things in our lives."

Lois Davis

GUTTENBERG, IOWA, USA

Photos by: Sara Davis

RAEED MOHAMMAD ABDULAH

Raeed is a guide in Petra, Jordan.

> *"Love is Allah."*
>
> Raeed Mohammad Abdulah
> PETRA, JORDAN

KORIE ROBERTSON

Korie is a reality TV star on A&E's *Duck Dynasty*. Korie's goal in life is to spread love with her family, friends, community, and company.

> *"1 Corinthians 13:4 sums up love for me: 'Love is patient, love is kind. It does not envy, it does not boast, it is not proud. It is not self seeking, it is not easily angered. Love never fails.'"*
>
> Korie Robertson
> MONROE, LOUISANA, USA

IKARO VALDERRAMA

Ikaro is from Colombia and speaks fluent Spanish, Russian and English. We spent seven hours together on a bus to Olkhon Island. He is a poet, traveler, and musician who plays the Igil, an instrument from Tuvan, Siberia, Russia. Ikaro's tattoo says "Baikal" in Russian. The horse is a spiritual animal with the nomadic people.

"Love is the sound of your soul vibrating on the infinite."
Ikaro Valderrama
OLKHON ISLAND, RUSSIA

BUDDHA

"Hatred does not cease through hatred at any time. Hatred ceases through love. This is an unalterable law."
Buddha

Photo by: Benjamin Conley

BECKY FELDMAN

"Love to me means freedom, and connection and an energy that makes you feel connected to something outside of yourself and greater than yourself."

Becky Feldman

SANTA MONICA, CALIFORNIA, USA

MICHAEL KODOTHUWAKU

Michael met his wife, Chandra, 35 years ago when he started selling offering flowers in front of the Temple of the Sacred Tooth. He gave her little love notes when she visited his flower stall. They now have four children.

> *"Love is marriage and family."*
> Michael Kodothuwaku
> KANDY, SRI LANKA

Photos by: Chrissie Lam

> *"Love is a flower,*
> *you got to let it grow."*
> John Lennon
> LIVERPOOL, UNITED KINGDOM

JERIES (GEORGE) RAMOS HALIN

Jeries (George) is among a minority group of Arab Christians in Bethlehem. He loves Jerusalem and Palestine and hates no one. The only thing he hates is Candy Crush invitations on Facebook. He invited me to his grandma's house for lunch and took me to Church of Nativity.

"Love is something that makes humans happy. It's a good feeling."
Jeries (George) Ramos Halin
BETHLEHEM, PALESTINE

Photos by: Chrissie Lam

CAZMIR LEENHEER

"Love is sensitive and intelligent, but at the same time absolutely not."
Cazmir Leenheer
BERLIN, GERMANY

Photographer Spotlight

SEAN DEKKERS

One of my fondest experiences contributing to Love is Project was over two weeks of traveling with Chrissie to photograph artisan groups and nuns in the Kingdom of Bhutan. Bhutan is a paradise for those seeking intrigue, authenticity and a trip off the beaten path. Its natural beauty and preserved tradition make for an explorer's dream, while the backdrop of mountaintops adorned with prayer flags makes the experience nothing short of magical. From elaborate spiritual ceremonies in the public square to intimate gatherings of the home, Bhutan is rich with tradition and craft that is on full display. From the moment you set foot into the country, you are completely immersed in tradition in a way that feels completely unique.

Visiting Bhutan is a little like having a time machine. Every aspect of their culture has been preserved and done just as it has been done for the last thousand years. Bhutan has resisted the temptation to change and you can see it in every aspect of their culture. From traditional dress to wood carvings and ornate fabrics meticulously crafted by hand, Bhutan embodies reverence which is proudly on display in its temples, villages, and mountaintops.

Besides being one of the few hidden treasures left in the world today, the warmth of its people is what makes it a unique and special place. I think everyone needs to experience Bhutan once in their life.

Just as we all have transformational moments that leave us forever changed, Bhutan will change you and forever leave you seeing the world in a slightly different light. Bhutan was this for me, and being able to explore it with nuns, families, Chrissie, and Love is Project made it one of the most transformational trips that I've ever taken.

Sean Dekkers is a human-centered product designer and director bringing over a decade of transdisciplinary design experience with an expertise in product discovery, product development, design research and prototyping for digital and physical products. He has held design lead roles at IDEO, McKinsey, and Visa.

"Love is life…
and happiness."
Dawa Pemo
THIMPHU, BHUTAN

Photos (current/next page) by: Sean Dekkers

Photos by: Tommaso Riva

HOLI MOLI! FESTIVAL OF LOVE

"The soul becomes dyed with the color of its thoughts."
- Marcus Aurelius -

Every culture has its own unique way of waving goodbye to winter and welcoming spring. Hindus do it with an explosion of love and color during Holi, a multi-day festival that commemorates the goddess Radha's divine love for Krishna. On the last day, Rangwali Holi, revelers take to the streets to drench each other in colored powder, sing, and dance. The Holi Festival signifies the victory of good over evil, the arrival of spring, the end of winter, and—for many—a festive day to meet others, play, laugh, forget, forgive, and repair broken relationships. Above all, it is a celebration of love.

love is
spontaneous.

Photo by: Georgina Goodwin

LOVE IS SPONTANEOUS

---

*"Love is adventure. It can come from anywhere
and take you around the world."*
- Rheanna Colyer -

When was the last time you planned a trip and followed
it to a tee? The key to leading a meaningful and fulfilling
life, is to "go with the flow." Every time I changed plans
because a new opportunity popped up, I've never been
disappointed. In fact, had I not followed the power of
a single bracelet and abandoned my original life plan,
Love is Project would never have been born.

Photo by: Chrissie Lam

TAMAR ARESHIDZE

Tamar Areshidze is a 24-year-old designer.

"Love is beyond the borders of logic. It is inside you until someone comes along and reflects it."

Tamar Areshidze

TBILISI, GEORGIA

In 2014, while traveling for Love Is Project's photo project, Zissou—one of my dear friends from Bali—introduced me to his neighbor, Eiji. Eiji is the Japanese filmmaker responsible for the "Happy" documentary.

Later, in a serendipitous, small-world moment, I noticed a vintage photo of my new friend, Eiji, with a group of teens tagged on Facebook. Scanning over the other faces, I recognized a caption with the name "Dan Eldon." Dan was a young photojournalist who moved to Kenya when he was just seven years old, and was killed in Somalia in 1993. Unbeknownst to me, Eiji was one of Dan's best friends and had traveled with him.

Dan Eldon's journal, "The Journey is the Destination," served as a huge inspiration for me since college. Eiji and Dan's project inspired me to go to Kenya, which in turn, inspired the creation of Love Is Project—allowing me to serendipitously meet and profile Eiji 25 years later. Everything definitely happens for a reason!

> *"Love is compassion. There is a strong correlation between compassion and happiness—understanding joy and sorrow, and feeling moved to help."*
> Eiji Han Shimizu
> YOKOHAMA, JAPAN

PAVEL ZHUKOV

I spent the 4th of July on a Moscow-bound train along with a Russian hockey team. They had just won second place in a St. Petersburg tournament, coached by Igot Krysov. They taught me the phrase, "Davaj Vyppjem!" which means, "Let's drink!" They even gave me one of their jerseys!

> *"Love is life. No matter the current political climate in Russia, Russians are friendly and nice, and welcome Americans here with open arms."*
> Pavel Zhukov
> MOSCOW, RUSSIA

SARA DAVIS + VERONIKA KARTASHEVA

Veronika (Nika) was the lightest soul I've ever had the honor to meet. She floated! Even though she has moved on to her next journey, I can still feel her presence and her joy. I'm thankful to have been able to photograph such a woman.

> *"I become a different person in the water...activated, more open, and more like a child. I connect to others and the ocean with no limits."*
> Veronika Kartasheva
> KAMCHATKA, RUSSIA

LUCIA CARBINES

Lucia is a contortionist and aerial artist based in Sydney, Australia. She gave us an impromptu performance during a TEDxUbud brunch.

"For me, love is that deep connection, whether it be between two people or something special. Where everything else just fades away, and you are completely absorbed and captured in that moment."

Lucia Carbines
NEW BRIGHTON, NEW ZEALAND

Photo (left) by: Sara Davis, Photo (above) by: Tânia Araújo

Photographer Spotlight

TOMMASO RIVA

I'm an Aries, born in Italy. I always felt like travelling and was never afraid to discover new worlds. Photography came into my life when I was 16, but I didn't realize it. I was too busy thinking about jazz music, which was my first real love. Then I studied economics and worked in finance.

When I moved to New York 12 years ago, I started to feel the urge to take photographs of jazz scenes. It came like lightning. I never had a previous interest in photography. There was no Instagram and very few iPhones, so it was a great time to take pictures. I decided to quit my nine-to-five job, which felt like a cage.

I moved back to Milan and started working in photography. I tried everything I could, but somehow I ended up really liking interior stories and shooting people in a very natural way. When I moved to Bali five years ago, I discovered a whole new world and fell in love with the eccentric architecture.

I met Chrissie while in Bali. She liked my natural style and we did some amazing shoots together. We made a huge mess every time, playing with colors, flowers, powders and fake ice. It always turned out well. My work outside of Love is Project is mostly around interiors and stories about interesting people.

I love my work as it allows me to discover hidden, magical worlds, meet interesting people, hear their stories, and always learn something new.

Tommaso Riva is an Italian photographer based in Bali. His work has been published in Elle Decor, Officiel, Living Corriere, Vogue Living, Belle, Design Anthology and Departures.

"Love is impermanence."
Tommaso Riva
ITALY

JESSICA KAMELL

*"May all beings be peaceful and free
and may my own words, thoughts and
actions conribute in some way to that
happiness and freedom for all."*

Jessica Kamell
BALI, INDONESIA

Photos by: Chrissie Lam

LOVE IS BORDERLESS

In August 2014, tourism to Petra, Jordan, had come to a standstill due to regional conflicts. The UNESCO site which normally hosts 5,000 visitors a day, now barely had 300. Traveling by donkey, my guide took me cave-hopping to meet the inhabitants of the modern day Bedrock. If you're Bedouin, you can stake your claim on any empty cave in Petra and make it your home—put doors in, paint the interiors, even park your car in the cave garage. No rent. No mortgage. You don't even have to ask any one! As a former New Yorker, this is an unfathomable concept.

I shared tea with the Bedouin patrol team at sunset overlooking Petra. Ahmed self-tattooed his beloved's name, Miriam, on his arm before she agreed to marry him. He's happy she said "yes." They now have five children. "Love is the best thing in life." For Mahmoud, who has six kids, "Love is a feeling that describes no borders."

After a meal at my guide's village, I went road tripping with Ahmed and Mahmoud. I asked them to play me their favorite tune in the car. Expecting local music, I was surprised when they turned the volume up on "Gangnam Style" and sang along to every word. Apparently, love is K-pop in Jordan.

Photographer Spotlight

ANNA WATTS

My adventure with Love Is Project began by Lake Atitlán, Central America's deepest lake (no one really knows how deep it is—rumor has it that the ruins of an abandoned Maya town can be found at the bottom) and renowned as one of the world's most beautiful places. Atitlán is never short of breathtaking, even if the 20-plus Guatemala stamps in my passport suggest I've been there a few too many times.

At Lake Atitlán, I met Chrissie, founder and CEO of Love Is Project, who hired me for a whirlwind photoshoot across several locations. In the true "Love Is Project way" (embrace the world!), Chrissie and I planned a day of lifestyle shooting that would bring us to three of these different communities (with seven models from four different countries!) by way of the typical transport used to get between towns around the lake: *lancha* or boatride. One of our stops on this journey was an artisan village farther along the lake—San Antonio Palopó.

There, we met a group of artisans who were crafting all Love Is Project Guatemala bracelets, hand weaving these beautiful pieces on small foot looms with threads purchased in local textile shops. This group of artisans are Kaqchikel Maya and most speak only the indigenous language of Kaqchikel. We had a lot of fun sharing and translating Kaqchikel and Spanish definitions of love before observing the intricate process of weaving that would produce the "Love Is" Guatemala bracelets. The San Antonio Palopó group of artisans were curious, but very shy—it was the first time they'd ever been in contact with a camera like mine.

Anna Watts is a documentary photographer and visual storyteller based in Brooklyn, NY and often in Central America. Watts is committed to ethical storytelling, using her work as a tool to advocate for sustainable, empowering change within indigenous and marginalized communities.

LOVE and a Tale of Two Cities

Photos by: Lise Honsinger, Danielle Rubi, Lionel Gasperini, Illustration by: Vannina Olivieri

In 2015, I had a vision of bringing strangers together to document LOVE in the "City of Love." The "Je suis Charlie" terrorist attacks just one month earlier had lingered in my mind. I believed our Love Is Project message could be a powerful statement of love and tolerance.

Just two weeks before our trip, I organized a gathering of photographers, videographers, artists and students for a Love is Project takeover. Being greeted by a mixture of friends, friends of friends and strangers in Le Marais touched me beyond words. Love filled the week as each collaborator explored the meaning of love in Paris.

I had chatted about the Paris takeover with Roger Markfield, the then-chairman of AEO.

He suggested we also visit London to execute the same concept. A week later, we were in London, profiling residents and tourists alike to find out what love means to them. What follows are a few of the answers we received, and a portrait of love in these two iconic cities.

> *"Our Love is Project message could be a powerful statement of love and tolerance."*
> Chrissie Lam
> SAN FRANCISCO, CALIFORNIA, USA

MARI + MANOLO

This photo was taken one day after Mari and Manolo of Spain got engaged by the Eiffel Tower. We met on the Love Locks bridge as they were attaching their lock.

"Love is very important to us and all of life. Love is life, happiness and celebration."

Mari + Manolo

BARCELONA, SPAIN

SAPANA AGRAWAL

Sapana Agrawal is passionate about healthcare and believes in giving a voice to people who don't have the most basic of care. She loves having her family here with her in London.

"Love is safety, passion, and hope."

Sapana Agrawal

LONDON, ENGLAND

ANGIE ALLGOOD RAE + MARK RAE

Angie Allgood Rae and her husband, Mark Rae, have now been together for over seven years. Mark loves Angie's energy and Angie loves Mark's sense of humor, intelligence and compassion. He proposed at night on the beach in Northumberland. He is a renowned music producer and screenwriter. They met on a Malibu beach. She was running an event while he was fishing. They didn't see each other for a year, then reconnected. The rest is history.

Photos (clockwise from left) by: Jamison Monroe, Chrissie Lam, Erin Burke

"Love is a commitment to growth through thick and thin...learning how another person wants to enjoy life and helping to grow that. We provide a good balance for each other. Love is also leaving the last biscuit in the tin for the person you love."

Angie Allgood Rae
LONDON, ENGLAND

MODE HUNTER

"Love is someone to share everything with plus unconditional acceptance."

Mode Hunter
PARIS, FRANCE

love is resillient.

Photo by: Sean Dekkers

LOVE IS RESILIENT

"Love is a choice in the darkest and lightest of times."

\- Touline Habake -

DAMASCUS, SYRIA

All of life's setbacks sting—it's the things we couldn't plan for, or maybe sensed were coming, but couldn't control. During my travels and while running Love is Project, many, many things did not go as planned. I've learned that love is a battlefield... sometimes. To love is to learn how to let people go.

Photos by: Georgina Goodwin

JULIANI

Juliani is a musician who was born on the streets of Dandora Slum.

> *"Being a musician is hard, but you have to work. Love is a choice. It goes beyond the eyes and the feelings. It goes deep down—that precious rock you have to get dirty to get to. You have to work...get your hands dirty. First yourself, and then the commitment."*

Juliani

NAIROBI, KENYA

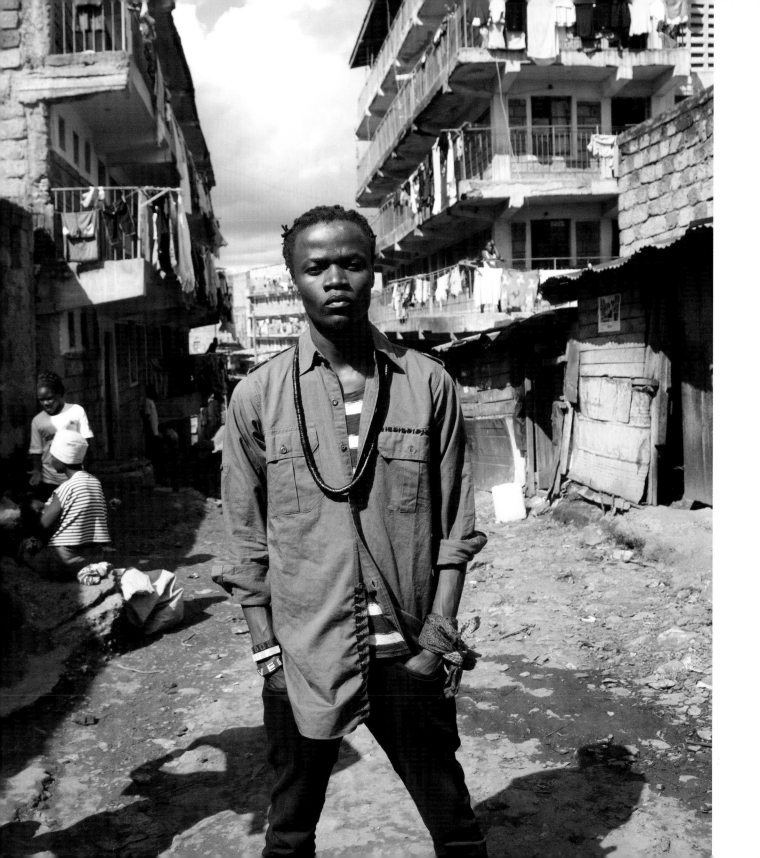

Photo by: Chrissie Lam

SHIAO-YIN

Shiao-yin is a serial entrepreneur from Singapore as well as the youngest person in the Parliament. She started The Thought Collective, which encompasses three Food For Thought restaurants in the city, School of Thought, Think Tank, Scape Journeys and Common Ground.

"Love is sacrifice. It sounds like a soft word but it's not. It is really tough. Love is resilience. It is enduring and persevering even when the situation is hard and the other person is being unloving. When you don't want to love, but you choose to love still... only then will you have finally grasped what love really is."
Shiao-yin
SINGAPORE

Photo by: Chrissie Lam

PETER PRATO

This typewriter was given to him by an ex-girlfriend he isn't in touch with anymore. For him, it's a reminder of the reach of a spirit of a person.

> *"Love is staying up all night long with another human being who's in pain so that they don't have to experience it alone."*

Peter Prato
SAN FRANCISCO, CALIFORNIA, USA

VANNINA OLIVIERI

Vannina is an illustrator based in Corsica, France who collaborated with Love is Project in Paris.

LAUREN HOTSON

"Love is infinite life force energy, the intelligent creator. Love is unconditional. Love is what we are when we are stripped back to our purest essence. Pure love is love of oneself."

Lauren Hotson

SYDNEY, AUSTRALIA

Photographer Spotlight

WAWAN MUHAMMAD

It is not easy to describe what love is using words. I am not a poet and I am not a writer. I am a hobby photographer. I work full-time as a humanitarian aid worker, serving men, women, and children affected by war, conflict or natural disasters.

Love, for me, is the joy I feel when I see the excited face of a little girl receiving a new school bag, books and pencils. Love is the hope I see from her little eyes when she realizes that the next day she can go to school with her friends to study and play, even if she is still living in a refugee camp. Love is the resilience that she brings to the world. Love is real, and I witness it every day.

Wawan is a humanitarian aid worker from Indonesia with a passion for photography. He is a believer in true love and unicorns!

DAW PIKE

Daw, 73, has rolled cigars for 53 years. Her family wanted her to help grow sesame, but she liked making cigars better. These cigars consist of palm tree wood mixed with tobacco and rolled in corn husks. The tradition has been in her family for over 100 years. Daw's husband grew up in the same village as her, so she knew him as a child. The romance started when they rode a bull cart into town. She married him at 19.

Daw's husband died 40 years ago and she has been taking care of the family ever since. She never remarried. She has five children—three of which are now deceased—and more than 20 grandchildren. Her daughter recently died, and her grandson, pictured here, now lives with her.

Photos by: Chrissie Lam

"Love is worrying. I worry about those I love."

Daw Pike
BAGAN, MYANMAR

MAHMOUD

Mahmoud is from Aleppo, Syria and has lived in Germany for two years with his second wife. He can't read or write, but he comes to school every day to "write and write... like a painter." It is his own personal endeavor. He can cook and makes a special Turkish dessert, Baklava, with marzipan and nuts. He loves to play with his grandkids.

"Love is community."

Mahmoud

ALEPPO, SYRIA

ART GIMBEL

Art united global festival communities. His passion was experiencing cultures around the world. He traveled extensively through 80 countries. Rest in peace, Art Gimbel. You are an inspiration. I will miss your love, laughs, creativity, puns, bear hugs, and zest for life and living.

"Love is embracing differences."

Art Gimbel

SAN FRANCISCO, CALIFORNIA, USA

Photos by: Chrissie Lam

CLAYRNE VAN ANTWERPEN

I met Clayrne from Holland on the train. It was the day after her birthday and one year since her husband of 20 years had passed away. She showed me his photo on her iPhone. She looked at it constantly throughout the trip and told me she misses him every day. The couple had previously traveled the world together. With the love of her life no longer around, love had now come to signify sorrow.

> *"Love is sorrow and grief."*
> Clayrne Van Antwerpen
> HOLLAND

RAGHEB + MOHAMMED

I had the opportunity to visit my friend's community initiative to integrate the hundreds of refugees from the Middle East and Africa outside of Frankfurt.

> *"If there is no love, there is no life."*
> Rabheb
> AFRIN, SYROA

> *"Love is home and family."*
> Mohammed
> AFRIN, SYRIA

Photos by: Chrissie Lam

Photo by: Julia Framcombe

TIRAS

Most Samburu moms are not literate. So, Tira—a Love Is Project artisan—has learned LOVE as a beadwork pattern. For the Samburu, the patterns in beadwork are a language in and of themselves. They reveal where they are from, if they are warrior girls, if they are married, and much more. The Samburu use the word *reto* to describe love—it means to uplift and to give strength. Drought, famine, and wars have plagued Northern Kenya. By offering more economic opportunities to Samburu women, we can create more stability. Love can end wars and bring peace.

"Love is loving someone the same way you love your child."

Tiras

LAIKIPIA, KENYA

LAURA WAITZE ZUCKERMAN

In 2018, Love is Project donated 1,600 bracelets to Marjory Stoneman Douglas High School in the wake of the deadly shooting there— offering a reminder of love to a community so recently plagued with grief and fear. Laura Waitze Zuckerman is a photographer in Parkland, Florida, the founder of Concert For Our Children, and the mother of students at Marjory Stoneman Douglas High School.

A bracelet may seem insignificant to some. But to me, Chrissie's bracelets were a tiny form of hope—hope in our society that some still love.

In this time of darkness, these bracelets with "love" written in different languages, touched me—if even for just a moment. I started to give them out to students, teachers, and anyone that I thought needed some love.

I am a local photographer, but after the tragedy, I couldn't pick my camera up. I had no desire to capture moments—those moments were too sad and heartbreaking.

It took some time and eventually, several months later, I started to photograph events that bring

Photo by: Laura Waitze Zuckerman

awareness to the awful epidemic of gun violence. I felt that in some small way, I was helping. Hopefully, anyway.

I met Michael Franti, an incredible musician, and gave him a love bracelet. I explained to him what Love Is Project is doing to spread love. He paused, stared at the bracelet, and gave me a heartfelt thank you.

I recently was photographing another local event—a new garden on the grounds of our high school. It was started by Tori, Joaquin Oliver's girlfriend. I introduced myself and told her that

this amazing woman, Chrissie, gave me some bracelets to help spread her message of love. Tori, who like everyone else, has shed enough tears recently to last a lifetime, smiled and put on the red LOVE bracelet.

These bracelets represent so many things, but I can tell you that for me, personally, they represent (and again, I know I am repeating myself) hope. Hope that one day love will triumph over hate. Hope that love is stronger than hate. And hope that one day, no one else will ever need to feel the sadness that has struck our town and the country as a whole.

Photographer Spotlight

BENJAMIN CONLEY

Benjamin Conley is a filmmaker/photographer living in Los Angeles, CA. He believes everyone has a story to tell. His passion is helping to bring those stories to life. He graduated from UC Berkeley in 2003 with a degree in American Studies and was an Honorable Mention All-Pac 10 baseball player.

> *"Love is making sacrifices for someone or something more important to you than yourself."*
>
> Benjamin Conley
> LOS ANGELES, CALIFORNIA, USA

BRITTANY TAKAI

"Love is a fire that both fuels us and burns us. We can feel our highest highs and lowest lows with the people and things we love. I can be over the moon giddy, happy, grateful, confident, and excited about surfing. Then it can make me feel scared, defeated, confused, and disappointed. But at the end of the day, love is what makes us feel alive and connected, and I will continue to let that fire lead me to the people and things I can't live without."

Brittany Takai

SANTA MONICA, CALIFORNIA, USA

VERANIKA NIKANAVA

Rest in peace, Nika. What a loss for the world. So talented, lovely, and gone way too soon. I feel fortunate that our paths were able to cross during your time here. Thank you for all your beautiful contributions to Love Is Project. You will be missed.

"What if love is not a feeling, but a practice? What if love is not just a gift like some of us might think, but hard work? It requires a lot of discipline, patience, concentration, faith and the overcoming of narcissism. And only those who can practice hard enough will have the honor to carry it for the rest of their lives."

Veranika Nikanava
BELARUS

"Love is when you can't control your feelings, no matter how hard you try. When you can't be stable, when you can't focus, when you can't switch it off."

Veranika Nikanava

BELARUS

Photos by: Veranika Nikanava

"In the end it will never be about who betrayed you back then, or who got the better diploma, who has more money in their bank account, or who loved you when you were 17... It will be about how many teeth are left to chew your food."

Veranika Nikanava

BELARUS

July 25, 2019.

We are leaving this place after spent here 2 nights. It was just me and my husband Piotr. It's our first trip as a married couple. We are con our journey — have no idea yet to This is probably the only place like in the world. What other remote shelters do you know exist in the world? Let's meet there? Huh!? feel free to send me email where we should all meet ne Who knows maybe we will beca best friends one day!

nikanavanika@gmail.com

Hope to meet you one day some else in this beautiful world.

Nika & Piotr. With love from Bel

YOU ON TRAIL

PIOTR & NIKA JUST MARRIED 7/19 ♡

PIOTR MARKIEŁAŬ

Piotr was Veranika Nikanava's husband. The following passage is a dedication to his late wife.

"I wrote to Nika, asking to see her film, Generation 328. It turned out she knew about me already, as she was preparing for the film's production. She said it would be fun if I came to New York. In two months she met me at the airport. We spent a month travelling, and it was amazing. I never felt so deeply in love with a person. We could talk about everything. Together, we could do anything. I went to Belarus and was back to her three months later. She met me with flowers.

We made the decision to marry easily, without much thought, because we were so sure of each other. Two weeks before our wedding, we got fired on the same day. In the evening, we already had a plan: in two weeks we were moving to Alaska. We had a wedding party on the roof. The next morning we set sail in a big hurry.

Our time in Alaska was unforgettable! We spent hours on the road waiting for a car under the scorching sun, warming each other in a sleeping bag at night, sharing everything. Free birds, we did everything we wanted. We were heading to the mountains when we, rather by accident, decided to turn onto the Stampede Trail. We spent two nights in Chris McCandless' bus and it was raining...

Nobody ever gave me as much love as she did. Maybe, except for my mother. Now, I can hardly believe the time I spent with Nika was real.

Piotr Markiełaŭ

BELARUS

love is
acceptance.

Photo by: Georgina Goodwin

LOVE IS ACCEPTANCE

"You, yourself, as much as anybody in the entire universe, deserve your love and affection."
- Buddha -

To lead a life guided by pure conviction is not as simple as it sounds. But to love who you are and encourage others to do the same, is a gift to the world.

We must develop a gentle curiosity and remain open-minded in all things that we do not understand. Let's celebrate those brave enough to step into the light and own their truth.

CORY HARTONO

Cory works as an architect and designer.

> *"Love is accepting yourself and accepting others. Love yourself."*
>
> Cory Hartono
> JAVA, INDONESIA

CLAIRE JOSEPH

"Love is the greatest healing therapy. Heal yourself by loving yourself in order to give love and be an instrument of love."

Claire Joseph

VENICE, CALIFORNIA, USA

EZRA MITCHELL

Ezra found his way to Bali by way of New York, San Francisco and Austin. He came to Indonesia searching for his father, leaving an engineering job behind.

"Love is born with true self love. From authentic love of self we are then complete to share that love with others without fear."

Ezra Mitchell

BALI, INDONESIA

EMILY PEREIRA

"Love is the ultimate permission; it's the freedom to explore our heart's wildest whims without fear of judgement."

Emily Pereira

MAL PAIS, COSTA RICA

BIANCA YUZON-HENARES

"Love is the frequency at which we resonate with our highest selves, the spark from which creation began, and the song our hearts were made to sing."

Bianca Yuzon-Henares

MANILA, PHILIPPINES

BAILEY HUNT

"Love is caring for someone. Love is magic."

Bailey Hunt

SALT LAKE CITY, UTAH, USA

Photo (clockwise from left)
by: Mark Nicdao, Stephanie
Clanton, Ryan Lawton

"LOVE is love is love is love is love is love is love is love cannot be killed or swept aside."
Lin Manuel Miranda
NEW YORK, NEW YORK, USA

"You only need a heart full of grace, a soul generated by LOVE."
Dr. Martin Luther King, Jr.
ATLANTA, GEORGIA, USA

Photos by: Chrissie Lam

MAYA

Maya is 57 and has four children. She also cooks a mean potato curry. Maya means "love" in Nepali.

> *"I am LOVE."*
>
> Maya
> ANNAPURNA, NEPAL

SUMMER MCKEEN

> *"To me, love means being accepted for who you are no matter what."*
>
> Summer McKeen
> EUGENE, OREGON, USA

DREW AND LESLIE BRUGAL

Drew and Leslie have known each other since kindergarten. He asked her out in the fifth grade by giving her his ID bracelet. Later that day she heard from friends that he was a ladies' man and had a reputation for kissing girls. She wanted nothing more to do with him after that, and gave the bracelet back the next day.

In 2000, they reconnected at their 25th high school reunion in Long Island, New York. After initially assuming he was still full of it, she changed her mind. Not long after, sparks began to fly and six months later Drew presented his fifth grade ID bracelet inside a Tiffany's box and asked Leslie to go steady. This photo was taken on their 12th anniversary. To them, love is being free to be yourself and knowing you won't be judged.

"Love is being free to be yourself."
Drew and Leslie Brugal
PALO ALTO, CALIFORNIA, USA

Photo provided by: Summer Mckeen

Photo by: Chrissie Lam

Photo by: Benjamin Conley

CANDICE DAVIS

"Love is knowing thyself. Through self knowledge all forms of love are possible. We can more accurately understand, assess and accept our own foibles and extend the same to others."

Candice Davis

SANTA MONICA, CALIFORNIA, USA

ALICE

Alice and Sudhira are friends from Italy who met at university five years ago. Alice is visiting Sudhira in London.

> *"There is no one like Sudhira… She is crazy, so unique. Love is visiting your friends."*
> Alice
> LONDON, ENGLAND

Photos by: Chrissie Lam

JEFFREY MARSH

Jeffrey is a prominent advocate for LGBTQ rights. He reached a turning point in his life in 1997 while in a bookstore in Philadelphia. A book entitled "There Is Nothing Wrong with You" by Cheri Huber caught his eye. This book inspired him to accept himself for who he is. His transformative time at a Buddhist monastery in California with Cheri led him to the path he is on now.

> *"Love is total acceptance. It starts inward…loving and accepting yourself."*
> Jeffrey Marsh
> NEW YORK, NEW YORK, USA

BEVERLEY

"My biggest love story has been learning to love myself. If we can't love ourselves, how can we love others? Self-care is so important and required—physically, mentally, and emotionally. There are days when I've been down on myself—frustrated and unhappy. During those times, I ask myself: What do I love and appreciate about myself? If I can't find anything, then I ask myself: What do I want to create for myself to build up the confidence to fall in love with myself again? As Oscar Wilde would say: 'To love oneself is the beginning of a life-long romance.'"

Beverley

SANTA MONICA, CALIFORNIA, USA

Photo by: Benjamin Conley

PIERA GELARDI

Piera, Co-founder of Refinery29,
celebrates PRIDE.

*"Love is old friends supporting
each other and watching each
other grow."*
Piera Gelardi
BROOKLYN, NEW YORK, USA

Photo (previous) by: Tomasso Riva, Photo (above/right) by: Chrissie Lam

SANDRA KELLER

*"Love is having compassion, giving
acceptance, remaining open, even when
it's hard. It isn't always easy, but it's
almost always worth the effort."*
Sandra Keller
WASHINGTON DC, USA

HOW BIG IS YOUR LOVE?

There are a lot of ways to get more involved in Love Is Project and support female artisans around the world:

- 1 -

Gift something special for yourself or someone you care about at **loveisproject.co**.

- 2 -

Get inspired with ways to show your love with our *Spread the Love* guide.

- 3 -

Follow us on Instagram (**@loveisproject**), Twitter (**@L0veisproject**) and Facebook (**@loveisproject.co**). Share your story and definition of love with us! Use **#loveisproject** to be featured on our page.

PRINCE OF PEACE FOUNDATION

POP's Foundation was founded in 1994 by Kenneth Yeung. It provides direction and funding to the Prince of Peace Children's Home (POPCH) in order to create a cheerful. loving, and nurturing environment for orphans with special needs. POPCH is the first official foreign-run children's home, a joint venture with World Vision China and the Civil Affairs Bureau of Wuqing, Tianjin, China.

POPCH welcomed its first group of 11 babies in 2003. The home now cares for more than 140 children, from infants to 18-year-olds. Among these are children with cerebral palsy, Down syndrome, autism, as well as various physical and intellectual disabilities. Since 2007, 51 of these children have been adopted by families in the United States, Belgium, Sweden, Spain, The Netherlands, and China.

Through the years, POPCH has dedicated staff and resources to provide the best possible rehabilitation services and medical care for each child. As a result, POPCH has earned numerous awards at the local, regional and national levels.

Your partnership with the Love Is Project will also help change the lives of the orphans at Prince of Peace Children's Home (POPCH).

ACKNOWLEDGEMENTS

It takes a village. This book and project is a labor of love and represents a compilation of the past five years. It has been a collaborative effort—and there are so many people to thank around the world. I appreciate everyone's hard work and contributions to Love Is Project. We couldn't have done this without all the initial Kickstarter supporters who made this book possible.

Massive thanks to my parents, Onsi & Gladys Lam, who supported me when Love is Project was in startup mode and worked tirelessly to see the project come to life. Hopefully, you can go back into retirement soon. My cousins, Kenneth Yeung and Amy Chung who helped sponsor the book. Shoutouts to Sean Dekkers for all his unconditional love and to Alan Omand, the Banson family, Yukswa Lau, Sophia Chen, and Kristin Cederholm. My Bali family, Bud Hart and the Hartland team: Wayan Lugra, Made, Nyoman, Koman, Darmie, Darma. Thanks to American Eagle Outfitters for initially getting behind Love Is Project when it was just an Instagram photo project.

Additional thanks goes to the contributing photographers who share their points of view: Georgina Goodwin, Tommaso Riva, Zissou, Sean Dekkers, Wawan Muhammad, Mark Nicdao, Jake Morales, Martina Orska, Pablo Naranjo, Lionel Gasperini, Chucho Potts, Khasar Sandag, Benjamin Conley, Sara Davis, Anna Watts, Bobby Neptune, Danielle Rubi, Peter Prato, Raskal, Tania Aranjo, and Nicole Gava.

Contributing illustrators: Sujean Rim, Vannina Olivieri, Amber Vittoria
Book cover designer: Gretchen Legrange
Book graphic designers: Grace Leong, Callie Lindsley
Copyeditors: Kristina Borza, Madison Hanna
Kickstarter video editor: Aaron Ekroth
Brand logo designer: Deena Suh

Thanks to all the friends and people I've met along my adventure who have graciously lent their faces and hands, or shared their prose for this book. It has been a long journey with many lessons learned along the way.

Lastly, a special thanks to all the artisans who have created for Love is Project. It has been wonderful to be able to connect and grow this concept of love across continents with your help.

Chrissie
xo

LIEBE AMOUR KÄRLEK CINTA
TÌNH YÊU AMOR 애정 AMORE
ਪਿਆਰ LOVE PAG-IBIG חב
ความรัก UPENDO LIEFDE
KÆRLIGHED ARMASTUS ÁST
DRAGOSTE ЛЮБОВЬ ՍԵՐ
DASHURI LÁSKA प्यार 爱

WHAT DOES LOVE MEAN TO YOU?

We've left a few pages blank for you to reflect on a love story of your own.

Be a part of *The Greatest Love Story Ever Told*.

....

....

....

....

....

....

....

....

SAMPLE PROMPTS

What does love mean to you?

How can I spread the message of love

... among family and friends?

... at my workplace?

... in my community?